Art & Science of Corporate Finance

A Practical Guidebook for FP&A Professionals

by
Kunal Malhotra

Disclaimer

This eBook is a work of nonfiction.

No part of this eBook can be transmitted or reproduced in any form, including print, electronic, photocopying, scanning, mechanical, or recording, without prior written permission from the author.

This eBook has been inscribed for informative and educational purposes only.

Every effort has been made to ensure that this eBook is as complete and accurate as possible. However, there may be mistakes in typography or content. Also, this eBook provides information only up to the publishing date, so it may not include some information about the author's life.

The purpose and objective of this eBook are to inspire, guide, and motivate others who want to achieve a successful career in the finance sector. The author and the publisher do not warrant that the information contained in this eBook is absolute and shall not be responsible for any errors or omissions.

The author and publisher shall have neither liability nor responsibility towards any person or entity concerning any loss or damage caused or alleged to be caused directly or indirectly by this eBook.

All Rights Reserved.

Copyright © 2022

Contents

Chapter 1 – The Corporate Finance Ladder   1

The Corporate Finance Sector   1

Financial Planning & Analysis (FP&A)   2

Primary Responsibilities   3

Budgeting and Forecasting   3

Rolling forecasts   4

Decision support   5

Special Projects   5

The Corporate Finance Hierarchy   6

Financial Analyst   6

Finance Associate   11

FP&A Senior Associate   14

FP&A Manager   15

FP&A Vice President/Director   17

Chief Financial Officer (CFO)   18

Chapter 2 – A Day in the Life of a CFO   19

The Right Hand of a CEO   20

The All-In-One Accountant, Business Leader, and Protector	23
More Than a Number Cruncher	23
Responsibilities at Hand	24
Shareholder Value Generation	25
The Role of the CFO in Leading Risk-Based Processes	25
Project Selection and Framing	26
Types of Risks and their Mitigations	26
Financial	27
Operational	29
IT	31
Miscellaneous & Unforeseen	33
Chapter 3 – The FP&A Lifecycle	**35**
Analysis	36
Business flow	36
Planning	41
Forecasting	43
Chapter 4 – Importance of Project Management Skills	**45**
Leadership	48
ROI Estimation	50
Ability to Delegate	51
Communication Skills	53
Research-Based Data Analysis	54
Financial Analyst and Cross-functional Stakeholders	55

Cross-functional Moves	57
Business Analytics: An Opportunity or Threat?	58
Chapter 5 – The Salary Guide	**60**
What Do FP&A Professionals Do?	61
The FP&A Career Path	62
FP&A Analyst	62
FP&A Associate	63
FP&A Manager	64
Director/ Vice President of FP&A	64
What's Next?	65
FP&A for People with Non-Traditional Profiles	66
Applicants for the Position of a Junior Analyst	66
Applicants for Managerial Positions in FP&A	67
Work-Life Balance	68
What to Expect?	68
Reasons to Work in FP&A	69
Chapter 6 - Having To Be Assigned The 'Special Projects	**71**
Market Research	72
Primary Research	73
Secondary Research	74
Optimization Of Process	75
Identifying Potential Targets (Mergers and Acquisitions)	76
Get Involved in The Early Stages	77

Rely On Past Experience	77
Review Transition Cost Estimates	78
Ensuring Information Is Unbiased	78
Allocation Of Capital	78
Strategic Capital Budgeting	79
Invest In Businesses Rather Than Projects	79
Assign Portfolio Roles into Capital Allocation Guidelines	80
Balancing The Investment Portfolio	80
Investment Project Selection	80
Think Out of The Box; Go Beyond Internal Rate of Return (IRR)	81
Chapter 7 – Benefits and Limitations of Financial Planning & Analysis	**82**
The Ability to Detect Patterns	83
A Chance to Budget Outline	83
Cash Flow and Income Review	84
Organization Liability Review	84
Audit Assets and Inventory	85
Distinguish Trends and Determine Steps Needed	85
Looking for Investment Capital	86
Smart Budget Allocation	86
Necessary Cost Reductions	87
Risk mitigation	88
Crisis management	88

It Acts as a Development Guide	89
The straightforwardness with Normal Staff and Finance Staff	90
Based on Market Patterns	93
At-One-Time Analysis	93
Forecasting:	94
Changes:	94
A Problem of Coordination:	95
Rapid Changes:	95
External and Miscellaneous Factors:	96
Time Consuming and Expensive Process:	96
Chapter 8 – How much of an Impact does FP&A have on a Company's Share Price?	**98**
Necessary Financial Statements for Every FP&A Team.	101
Budget Variance Analysis	101
Cashflow Forecasting	102
Executive Summary Reports & Dashboards Based on the Core Financial Statements	102
Operations Review Report	102
Chapter 9 – Upcoming Trends in Finance	**105**
Data and Processes Consolidation	106
Rely On Data Instead of Instincts	108
Precise Decision Making	111
Chapter 10 – The Exit Strategy	**113**

FP&A Exit Opportunities	113
Chief Financial Officer (CFO)	114
Chief Executive Officer (CEO)	114
Investment Banking	115
Corporate Finance	115
Controllership	116
Treasury	117

Chapter 1 – The Corporate Finance Ladder

The Corporate Finance Sector

Corporate finance deals with how organizations deal with their investment decisions, funding in the right places, and structuring capital the correct way through long and short-term financial planning, furthermore implementing these various financial strategies within the organization.

Corporate finance is concerned with maximizing shareholder value by making appropriate investment decisions. The finance department in any organization oversees a company's financial activities, whether to pay for a particular investment with debt, equity, or both or none. Such decisions generally keep the company's cash flow running.

Nevertheless, the authority of decision-making varies as per your position in a particular company. However, the primary goal remains to manage the company's finances by appropriately allocating the firm's capital resources. The cash surplus in projects is used to drive maximum revenue, payout dividends to shareholders, and pay back any creditor-related debt in the company.

Professionals in these large companies are not only responsible for working on deals; rather they are in charge of their ongoing operations while reporting these figures for cash management.

The three main areas at most companies when it comes to corporate finance are Financial Planning & Analysis, Controllership, and Treasury. Our scope of interest and focus in this book will be regarding the FP&A.

Financial Planning & Analysis (FP&A)

Financial Planning and Analysis (FP&A) is a sub-department within the finance department of a company and is responsible for understanding its historical background, analyzing the ongoing trends, and designing strategies that will impact its future performance. To instruct how business operations need to be in the future, the person/team needs to understand accounting and business operations. Most FP&A units are closely connected with other areas of the organization. Other organizational departments, including Sales, Marketing, Accounting, and Operations work closely with the FP&A team.

Primary Responsibilities

The primary responsibilities at hand are to create a strategic plan that will bring the senior management's vision to reality. The high targets that senior officials have in mind are not possible until somebody internally knows and understands the company. It is necessary to understand the gross revenue they generate, the net income they make, and what risks they can take without burning to ashes or just going through significant losses of any sort.

Budgeting and Forecasting

FP&A teams are responsible for using their analytical skills to create a budget for actual variance analysis. The purpose of this analysis is to provide answers to a series of questions that directly affect a company's operations.

Before forecasting for further months, and thinking of implementation strategies for the coming year, FP&A teams compare the performances according to various factors. When they reach the past and current year's performance, some questions arise, and they notice a pattern of changes.

For example, they might notice why the current year's expenses are higher than the previous year or which product/service leads to better performance when maximizing business operations.

Not only do these professionals report forecasts that they have gathered or analyzed through the collected data, but they also use that data to advise senior management on how to capture new opportunities. These teams are tasked with the development of the organization. As a vital part of the forecasting process, FP&A inevitably works on a series of special projects that vary from company to company in parallel with its set budget. FP&A would further develop an annual budget, where these teams are tasked with creating a rolling forecast.

Rolling forecasts

By definition, a rolling forecast predicts future numbers over a period by analyzing historical trends. It is a management tool that enables organizations to plan and forecast over a set time horizon and is often a part of financial reporting, planning & budgeting, and supply chain management across various departments within an organization. For example, if your company sets out its production calendar for a particular year, a rolling forecast will forecast the next months for you towards the end of that year.

Decision support

FP&A is not only responsible for the forecasts that they gather through thorough analysis, but they further use that data to advise the management on ways to increase efficiency and optimize growth.

The FP&A team is responsible for analyzing the set KPIs, forecasts with risks and opportunities, and a better plan that is identified to optimize performance to meet the set of goals. These professionals help the senior management to decide what would work best for the company's growth. The set goals need to be developed in line with real facts and figures. They need to have enough information to fight for the data they have collected and what they think is best for the company.

Special Projects

FP&A professionals must also provide their services for special projects that lie outside their domain of set targets. These special projects are time-consuming, but FP&A teams are often in the middle of these inefficiencies that they are tasked with helping and improving.

The Corporate Finance Hierarchy

The journey of the aspirational finance graduate begins as an analyst or as a banker. The initial grind pays off in big ways as the field is rich with growth opportunities that lead to a very satisfying and lucrative career. The road seems to end at the CFO position; however, as you will learn, that is not the be-all-end-all for someone in this industry. We will discuss here the hierarchical structure of a company's finance department, and of course, most importantly, how to move up the ladder. The most prominent roles in the FP&A sector that everyone will move through during their career are:

1. Financial Analyst
2. Financial Associate
3. FP&A Senior Associate
4. FP&A Manager
5. FP&A Vice President/ Director
6. CFO – Chief Finance Officer

Financial Analyst

For anyone starting their career in the finance sector, this is the first step. To become a financial analyst, often a bachelor's level university education is required, preferably in math, accounting, or finance.

Key Responsibilities

Although the role varies from company to company, often the primary role of financial analysts is to search for business opportunities and support running financial processes for reporting. Some newcomers feel that it is a baseline job and their opinion is not heard; this couldn't be further from the truth. As companies have to find ways to improve their portfolio and increase profit, they need the help of financial analysts to investigate investment opportunities and help navigate the company to make wise monetary decisions and mitigate stress and expenses.

As an accountant, you would gather raw experience in the industry that prepares you to tackle menial tasks head-on, like sheet balancing or auditing finances. As an analyst, those activities take the backseat, and you are studying and assessing investment opportunities, or understanding financial processes for reporting. Your responsibilities are to help guide your firm towards a more profitable future and be at the forefront of research and analysis.

Required Education

Any financial role is not rigidly tied to the needed education. You are not expected to be an expert in complex and advanced mathematical concepts. However, you should dedicate your time to studying and developing strong foundations in calculus, statistics, and algebra.

It is expected that someone in the position of a Financial Analyst at least holds a bachelor's degree. You can choose one of the following math or finance-related degrees that will help you get started and build a deep understanding of finance and accounting:

1. BBA – Bachelor of Business Administration
2. BSAF – Bachelor of Accounting and Finance
3. BS in Financial Mathematics
4. BS in Actuarial Mathematics

It may also make sense to pursue an MBA but is generally advised to those who have outgrown the current position and are willing to move up the corporate ladder.

The top courses you should take during your bachelor's degree other than the ones mentioned earlier are:

1. Accounting
2. Economics
3. Finance
4. Probability
5. Statistics and Statistical Inference
6. Derivatives
7. Auditing
8. Taxation

What about a Bachelor's degree in Data Science or Data Analysis?

One of the most sought-after degrees today is the BSDS (Bachelor of Science in Data Science). Even though it is most popular with those who have a background and interest in Computer Science, the Data Science degree focuses on the development of computational as well as mathematical and analytical skills. With the evolution of work, our worlds are overlapping more than ever.

Data Science is one of the best degrees to get started even if your focus is finance because it will help develop the necessary financial and accounting understanding, as well as help you get skilled with tools like predictive statistical models, machine learning, traditional statistics, data analysis, and data mining.

As a data scientist, you will stand out compared to a finance graduate, but if you are keen on developing better and more in-depth financial and mathematical, you should consider focusing on the already mentioned degrees and take courses on topics that are covered in the Data Science degree.

Required Skills

As mentioned earlier, skills matter more in the position of a financial analyst than formal education. This statement is not to undermine the importance of formal education, but once you are in the position or are being considered for the position of a Financial Analyst at any firm or company, these are the skills that are expected of you before you receive the position:

1. Clear mathematical concepts
2. Microsoft Excel, and PowerPoint
3. Ability to write detailed and well-researched reports
4. Excellent English without any grammatical errors in both speaking and writing

Skills to Learn at the Job

The position of a Financial Analyst will challenge you daily. The mundane activities of an accountant or banker do not apply here. Instead, you will be involved in learning about other businesses, seeking investment opportunities, and collaborating with fellow financial analysts on various projects or processes. The purpose of working anywhere is to learn new skills and the skills you will acquire over time as a Financial Analyst are:

1. Excellent, clear, and effective communication
2. Deep understanding of the stock market (if applicable)
3. Learn new financial products and services
4. Generally become better at deeply investigating and analyzing

5. Develop the ability to quickly and efficiently manipulate, and analyze numerical and statical data
6. Learn to manage time and stay organized
7. Grow specialized skills such as advanced Microsoft Excel

Expected Earnings and Salary

For anyone starting their career in the finance sector, money is undoubtedly one of their primary focuses. However, to set realistic expectations, the salaries for a Financial Analyst at any respectable firm or company is on average $72,000 per year (accurate up to March 2022). The good part of being in the finance industry is profit sharing. As you grow, so does the company. It is a directly proportional relationship that benefits both parties. Depending on the performance of the company overall and your input, you will be compensated with a share of the profit made, especially thanks to the financial advice you provide to your seniors.

Finance Associate

As your career progresses, and you have gathered about 3 to 5 years of experience as a financial analyst, it is time to climb one step up the corporate ladder and become a Finance Associate. Your responsibilities consist of diverse roles, and you help your superiors manage other finance officers.

Key Responsibilities

A Finance Associate develops accurate monthly and quarterly reports and investigates the hidden drivers within the business that contribute to variations in revenues and expenses. The Associate also provides detailed analysis and insights to their seniors and helps them improve the existing financial system in place by discovering pain points and discussing useful solutions and remedies.

Make sure to develop excellent reporting skills as this will help you move up in the corporate hierarchy and understand the internal working of the organization better. Recruiters require candidates for this position with excellent communication, management, and analysis skills.

Required Education

To become a Finance Associate, you need to know that most employers are looking for someone with a bachelor's degree along with some practical experience. I have already mentioned the bachelor's degrees you should consider pursuing if you are looking to start your career in finance. Most employers prefer those who have an MBA or a CFA (Chartered Finance Analyst) certificate or a CPA (Chartered Public Accountant) certificate.

Required Skills

For a Finance Associate, you need to be well acquainted with the following skills:
1. Expertise in developing detailed financial reports.
2. Excellent communication skills.
3. Expert-level English speaking and writing skills.
4. Excellent analytical skills.
5. Prior experience of a Financial Analyst.
6. Deep understanding and relevant experience in financial audits.

Skills to Learn at the Job

Even though you are expected to be a specialist and have expert-level skills in some areas, you still have a lot to grow. As a Finance Associate, your next step is to become an FP&A Senior Associate. Which means,

1. You will develop a deeper understanding of accountancy, financial, and operational principles.
2. You will develop stronger Microsoft Excel and PowerPoint skills.
3. You will develop sharp attention to detail.
4. The most important skill you will develop is to create perfect quality financial reports after examining set metrics.

Expected Earnings and Salary

    To set realistic expectations, the salaries for a Finance Associate at any respectable firm or company is on average $95,000 per year (accurate up to March 2022). With the aforementioned profit sharing, as you grow, so does the company. It is a directly proportional relationship that benefits both parties.

FP&A Senior Associate

    After about 5 to 7 years working in the finance sector, you have gained enough relevant experience to become a senior associate. A Senior Associate partners with the business unit's general managers and other senior directors.

Key Responsibilities

    The responsibilities of a Senior Associate increase significantly. A Senior Associate trains and teaches finance and operation teams assigned to them. Standing up and presenting to the senior executives is also a daily function.

Required Education

    A minimum of a bachelor's degree is needed to be a Senior Associate in any of the majors mentioned earlier.

Required Skills

As a Senior Associate, you are expected to have experience in all the above-mentioned skills as a financial analyst.

Skills to Learn at the Job

As an FP&A Senior Associate, you will develop senior-level skills in analysis, and your focus will be on forecasting and future budgeting.

Career Opportunities, Expected Earnings, and Salary

The position of a Senior Associate is a demanding one and quite rewarding. Senior Associates can expect a salary up to $115,000 a year (as of March 2022).

FP&A Manager

The FP&A Manager takes charge of business forecasting. In a smaller company, this role is filled by the owner and is the highest position. However, in a larger organization, the FP&A Manager is the leader of a complete unit.

Key Responsibilities

As an FP&A Manager, your responsibilities are to manage your team of financial analysts, associates, and senior associates. Mostly, in large organizations, a controller handles financial accounting, and the manager is the one in charge of management.

If you are the sole manager, your responsibilities are to do both, manage the team, as well as handle financial accounting.

Required Education

A minimum of a bachelor's degree is needed to be an FP&A manager in any of the majors mentioned earlier. You should be holding an MBA in Finance if you want to secure your position as an FP&A Manager.

Required Skills

All of the skills mentioned above, including communication, management, reporting, and analysis skills.

Skills to Learn at the Job

As a manager, you will be tested to your limits to manage and create harmony within the team. You need to act calm all the time and the skills you learn as a manager will apply everywhere as you climb the corporate hierarchy ladder.

Career Opportunities, Expected Earnings, and Salary

As an FP&A manager, you should be expecting an average salary of about $130,000 per year.

FP&A Vice President/Director

Key Responsibilities

As a vice president or director, you are responsible to lead the entire department responsible for planning, budgeting, forecasting, and reporting.

Required Education

You should at least have an MBA in Finance if you want to secure your position as the VP of an FP&A and it is better to have an MBA, CPA, or CFA certificate.

Required Skills

All of the above skills including management, communication, and performance analysis.

Career Opportunities, Expected Earnings, and Salary

The next steps from being a vice president can be anyone of the following:

1. You either land a position *as* the CFO after years of proven experience and a track record of excellent business decisions.

2. You are offered to be the CEO of the firm if you have an excellent reputation and relationship with the employees, your business decisions and leadership have moved teams towards higher

success, and you are capable of taking charge of an entire company.

3. You are appointed the President of the company to deal with upper management matters and provide cohesion and make great business decisions.

As VP, you will most definitely be making six figures, and in some cases and top companies, VPs make seven figures. This can vary from industry to industry.

Chief Financial Officer (CFO)

And finally, we have the highest position that one can attain in the corporate finance sector – the chief financial officer. I will discuss the CFO position in greater depth and detail in the next chapter that is dedicated entirely to this position.

Chapter 2 – A Day in the Life of a CFO

The ulterior motive of a company is to generate revenue and earn a profit. These profits are earned when the operations in a company are being carried out accordingly. When we learn how an organization's hierarchy works, we understand how a company's CEO is the most important person. In contrast, big companies and corporations do not run because of one person alone.

All in all, it is a combined team effort since the revenue that comes in is because of how a team has performed and provided a remarkable service.

Yes, the CEO is the most important person in every organization. But the second most important person is the CFO, who looks after all the accounting and finance-related activities. From a broader perspective, there is so much more to the responsibilities he has for himself. You need to be articulate and judiciously manage the money you make, and that is the reason why the CFO position is so indispensable. Furthermore, a CFO provides financial analysis for the future through a systematic process. The CFOs make the most necessary contribution as improved business performance while leading to increased profitability by covering all allotted costs.

The Right Hand of a CEO

Can you take the ridiculous complexities of modern finance and put them into a language that the normal audience can understand either in writing or through slides? If the answer is yes, you have what it takes for the CEO to trust you to keep the company's financial wheel moving.

Necessary skills like in-depth knowledge of financial concepts and a tight grasp on implementation of those concepts are immensely essential.

Whereas if you are aiming to be the CFO of an organization, there is a set of skills that you need to hone to run an organization's processes effectively.

According to Alister Cowan – CFO of Suncor Energy, North America's 7th largest integrated oil company,

"As your career starts, you're generally very technical, resulting in your early promotion being primarily due to technical strength. But to be the CFO of an organization, you need to know more than just the technical bits. As you move more into senior roles like the CFO, leadership skills increase prominence."

The CFO needs to have:

1. Business understanding
2. Communication skills
3. Relationship-building skills
4. Finance team builder

- **Business acumen:**

To be a good financial advisor as well as strategist one needs to have comprehensive knowledge of the core business of the organization. Hence, a good CFO knows enough to walk the floor and understand the business beyond the numbers since by the time you dig up numbers, they are old, and there is little that can be done about it. To be in the CFO position, you need to see outside of what the statistics tell you and be prepared for uncalled storms that may throng your way anytime.

- **Key to a good relationship – Communication:**

One skill that we find missing from the CFO's in-power is strong communication skills: reference from conducted research. This includes both written and verbal communication skills. You can't possibly circulate financial information without some commentary and expect people to reach good conclusions. CFOs with great communication skills are the face of the company when discussing its financial health on media.

- **Trust works:**

    The most important relationship that you need to build is first with the CEO. It strongly needs to be based on trust's basic virtue with relevance to the Lencioni trust pyramid relationship. Building relationships proactively needs to be the fundamental key here. CFO needs to get the conversation going with the CEO and develop relationships with peers, investors, and colleagues. CFOs who can budget the time to seek peers, team members, and employees will have a much stronger sense of the business's operational aspects.

- **A support system:**

    The key to effectively managing the key processes in a business is to recruit the right kind of people who share the same vision as you. Your support system needs to efficiently deal with various compliance issues at hand while simultaneously participating and maintaining strategy.

    The CFO will need to help their team understand the business better so that they can have a better enterprise.

The All-In-One Accountant, Business Leader, and Protector

When a finance professional moves from budgeting, financial reporting, and control to becoming a so-called strategic partner: also a major responsibility of being a CFO, it serves as moving one step up the ladder. You are now a 55% accountant, 25% business leader, and 20% protector. The CFO mandate is much broader.

You are not just responsible for monitoring and reporting numbers; you are also responsible for managing the people and making sure the financial wheel runs smoothly. These people are passionate about two things; winning and business (bringing the money on board). Hence, while they are great strategic thinkers, they can greatly impact implementing strategies while being technologically advanced.

More Than a Number Cruncher

A CFO has evolved from being just a number cruncher to having a seat at the table as a strategic thinker. He now gets to sit along with the board and the CEO to develop the right strategies while being the voice on the practice's financial performance.

A CFO contributes to the profitable growth of the company through efficient and effective financial solutions.

As businesses have evolved into a more dynamic nature, CFOs are expected to be business partners and enablers for growth, whereas they weren't given as much respect in the past as compared now.

While these business processes are in practice, CFOs must rely on and understand the numbers of the past and predict the future while maintaining a scientific, data-driven, and objective decision-making nature.

These decision-makers have now progressed enough to get a prestigious seat at the table, which was never the case earlier.

Responsibilities at Hand

With more representation at the table comes greater responsibility. The seat next to the CEO as a valid decision-maker requires strategy development and an understanding of the business's mechanics. This is why you will notice many great CEOs were initially CFOs of an organization.

It's the people skill you learn while managing finances that lead to a higher authority in an organization.

As CFOs became more comfortable with digital technology, they gravitated toward strategic decisions that impact technology deployment. Now, instead of just controlling which money goes where, they find value in digital transformation.

Shareholder Value Generation

Guiding the business model choice that companies will adopt is decided as a team when the business sources are discussed. The key factor to keep in mind as a decision-maker is to carry forward the assets that maximize value. This falls under the CFOs umbrella as a strategic thinker to analyze what drives maximum revenue. It is like picking and choosing your apples for a higher turnover.

The Role of the CFO in Leading Risk-Based Processes

"Risk comes from not knowing what you're doing."

– Warren Buffett

The CFO implements risk-based planning processes to generate value and enable growth. Every business organization focuses on substantial growth and maximum profit. Every step that you take, and every move that you make somehow, is to optimize more cash flow. In an outsourced company, venture-based company, startup, or private company, a CFO's role involves having a series of responsibilities that he/she needs to ensure for the company's development.

Several areas where active management and leadership are required to lead, coach, and support these processes to generate value-added insights are:

Project Selection and Framing

The starting point is to ensure that you choose projects appropriately. The right selection of the project plays an important factor in ensuring any initial applications of ideas. As a CFO, when you select a project, you make sure that the idea generates cash flow and adds value to the company by not just being a box-ticking exercise on risk management. New thought processes and techniques need to be implemented with every project, and every production assessment needs to be different from your last.

Once you have chosen a project (or projects), you need to create a proper structure and guide. You have to appoint the guidance of your financial project managers on your projects to ensure their timely completion.

Types of Risks and their Mitigations

As a CFO, you are responsible for choosing projects that align your risk management strategies, and with set business goals. When you can make the right decisions when it comes to dealing with risks, you create a dialogue with other stakeholders and decision-makers to choose the best set of techniques that can drive the results most effectively and maximize the project's benefits, i.e., cash flows or resource savings, etc.

Financial

(i) Financial Compliance

The compliance for a company slightly varies based on the fact if it is a publicly-traded company or a privately-owned company. The requirements for complying with the rules and regulations of their residing state need to be followed with utmost discipline. As a CFO, you will be held responsible for any taxation and revenue statements and if you fail to comply, the entire company will be at risk of collapse and there'll be serious fire from the shareholders, law enforcement agencies, and regulators.

(ii) Debt

The collection of capital can be done in many ways. Essentially, until the investors and lenders have not been paid back fully including the promised profit or shared loss, that capital is a loan or debt.

If the company has taken a loan, it is important to return it as soon as possible to avoid penalties and extra charges. The CFO is responsible for keeping track of all of the pending payments, including any expenses and bills. Failure to do so can result in severe class action lawsuits for the company.

(iii) **Liquidity**

One of the biggest challenges that CFOs face is to investigate and understand the entire cash flow of an organization. There are plenty of issues that arise with where cash needs to be placed or invested at a specific time. The most difficult choices come from deciding how to attain liquid cash, as well as where to invest that liquid cash where it cannot be frozen in a state that is unusable and is causing cash shortages.

(iv) **Mergers and Acquisition**

As your company grows in scale and it is looking to further increase its portfolio of companies and businesses under its belt, it may explore opportunities to merge and acquire other companies in the process. There are plenty of risks associated during these times and the CFO's responsibility is to evaluate and look deep into the investments, cash flows, payments, taxes, contracts, projects (complete or otherwise), employees and their financial standings, expenses, source of capital and any other financial related risks that the company has.

Operational

(v) Process

The way that a company operates depends on the processes, procedures and workflow it has designed for itself to follow. These processes are incorporated to reduce and mitigate any errors and risks associated with them. Regular scrutiny, analysis, and improvement of these processes are what ensure that the company does not fall into trouble and potentially cause harm to itself. The CFO is required to be fully aware of such processes and needs to coordinate with the project managers to ensure that they are not facing any friction.

(vi) Operational Compliance

Based on the industry and sector your company operates in, you will have a specific process and operational rules and regulations to follow and comply with. It is important for companies to not have a public image of providing subpar quality products that are a result of poor management and operational issues. The CFO needs to be well aware of the regulations needed to be in place while these processes are operational.

(vii) Workforce

The company is essentially its workforce. With no one to work with, you won't get any work. The risks wildly vary but essentially, the issues that universally revolve around the company's workforce have to do with any one of the following: The economy could be struggling and people are being laid off to deal with expenses better. The economy is performing well and the workforce is quitting for better and higher-paying opportunities. Although salary is one of the issues that dictate how the workforce feels about their work, the other issue is the relationship between the employees.

(viii) Supply chain

Companies that sell physical products are involved with a properly structured supply chain. There is plenty of risks involved with the uncertainty of the flow and movement of products from one location to another. Resource allocation and management are the primary part of the supply chain that then move to the processing stage. For example, if you are the manufacturer of garments, your company solely relies on the supply chain of getting raw materials such as wool and cotton. If you cannot manage to have enough for a specified day to fulfill manufacturing, you will suffer production loss if you have not adequately managed the storage of these raw materials. If these issues revolve around payments, then the CFO needs to be involved immediately to eliminate the issue.

IT

(ix) IT Compliance

The rules and regulations within the residing state apply to the IT department of your company. Not only that, but it is also important that the workforce complies with the internal rules and regulations of the company's IT department. IT compliance is the primary concern of European companies as the GDPR (General Data Protection Regulation) kicks into gear wherever IT is involved. Failure to comply can have dire consequences. Similar rules and regulations apply based on your regional presence and vary slightly. IT compliance is not strictly limited to companies that provide IT services, as every company needs a dedicated IT department. The CFO needs to be aware of the IT compliance of the company, as failure puts everyone in jeopardy and can result in loss of revenue. There are plenty of steps that can be taken, but make sure that in the pursuit of compliance, you do not end up breaking any rule or regulation that can get you in trouble. For example, if you wish to prevent employees from accessing certain websites, or you wish to lock access to the USB ports on company-provided computers, then instead of taking dubious actions like allowing these activities but monitoring the data, it is better to ensure they are not allowed through the establishment of firewalls.

(x) Security

As mentioned earlier, the GDPR is dedicated to protecting the privacy of the data of its citizens. It is a must for everyone in European countries to comply with the GDPR which is implemented on a continental level. The purpose of the GDPR is not just compliance but also to implement security and safety of the citizens. In the US, a similar regulation of CDPA is in effect to protect consumers. In addition, there are plenty of IT-related security threats and risks including (but not limited to) ransomware attacks, DDoS (Distributed Denial of Service) attacks, server infiltration, forgery, piracy, data theft, publicization of private and hidden data, hardware failures (server and user level), etc.

(xi) Reliability & Availability

If you wish to have a healthy and operational company, then the importance of the IT department cannot be overlooked. As the CFO, you need to be aware of the site availability and service reliability of your IT department so that other employees do not feel restrained or feel that the services are not up to the required quality. Any delay in work can cost the company heavily.

Miscellaneous & Unforeseen

(xii) Natural Disasters

Depending on where your business is situated in the world, you could face several types of natural disasters (like hurricanes, sandstorms, earthquakes, floods, tsunamis, etc.). Other than natural disasters, your company can be a target of robbery, theft, terrorism, fires, etc. Your business should have measures ready in place to tackle these issues head-on and enough cash to help recover.

(xiii) Geopolitical

Depending on the country or state you live in, your business will be affected by the political environment of that location. You cannot be unaware of the political climate as that directly influences market conditions and stock prices. Since the political climate of the United States affects everyone globally, it is also important to be aware of it as much as possible. Some companies work internationally, meaning that they have multiple headquarters, and if the two countries they operate in go into a trade war or ban, you could be seeing severe damage and operational problems.

Chapter 3 – The FP&A Lifecycle

The primary functions of an FP&A team in an organization are to perform budgeting, forecasting, and analysis to give support to the CEO and CFO in making business decisions. The processes that they perform can be seen in the cycle illustrated below.

[1]

Let's go over the entire cycle in-depth below.

---

1 Retrieved From: https://corporatefinanceinstitute.com/resources/careers/jobs/financial-planning-and-analysis-fpa/

Analysis

The starting point of an FP&A cycle is 'Analysis'. For an FP&A department to be successful, it needs to have a strategy. An FP&A strategy helps and guides you to move in the direction you need to take your company in a given timeframe.

There is a financial analysis cycle which is illustrated below where I will discuss in each part how the financial analysis of a company is done.

Business flow

When you start a business, you need money for investment which is called 'capital' in financial terms. There are two ways to arrange capital, one is to invest your personal savings and the money you own, and the other method is to borrow money from reliable investors like a bank, friend, or capitalist.

The second step is to utilize that capital and acquire fixed assets. Fixed assets can be machinery, real estate, tools, etc. The next logical step is to take advantage of the assets and produce goods. Goods are any products that the company has expertise in producing and developing and can be sold for generating revenue. The financial term for the total amount of goods sold is called 'turnover'.

Depending on the nature of business, it is possible to sell goods on credit to your customers. One critical aspect of financial analysis is the investigation, specifically of loan or credit which is to make sure if it has been received from the company's customers or not. Most financial discrepancies or auditing issues arise from "missing money", and most of the time, that money is not stolen or lost; the company has not asked the customer to return the loan/credit.

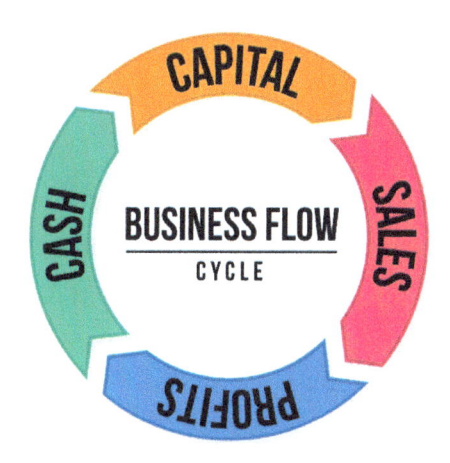

CAPITAL → SALES → PROFITS → CASH (BUSINESS FLOW CYCLE)

As illustrated above, you can see the business flow of any company.

Below, I have tried to explain some important financial ratios used in many industries, though they may differ depending on your particular industry. Starting with "Fixed Asset Turnover Ratio":

You arranged and invested capital, acquired assets, produced goods, sold goods, received profit, and reinvested. Fixed Asset Turnover Ratio shows if you are utilizing your assets to the best possible potential to produce those goods and maximize profit. The ratio tells you the efficiency of the whole process and is one of the most important parts of financial analysis. The ratio can simply be calculated by:

$$\text{Fixed Asset Turnover Ratio} = \frac{\text{Turnover}}{\text{(Net Fixed Assets)}}$$

If the ratio results in <1, then you are underperforming and potentially losing money. If the ratio is =1, you are at breakeven. The situation you need to be in is that your ratio should be >1, and the greater the number, the better your company is performing.

Net Profit Margin Ratio

The next ratio is called "Net Profit Margin". This ratio is used to calculate how much profit was generated by a unit of sale. A unit is decided depending on the scale of the company and the stream of cash. The standard unit is $1, but as mentioned earlier, can be a different number. So, net profit, in the simplest of terms, is how many cents of profit is made for every $1 worth of product sold. The net profit ratio needs to take into consideration every expense and only calculate the pure profit out of every sale. This ratio is calculated by:

$$\text{Net Profit Ratio} = \frac{\text{Net Profit}}{\text{Turnover}}$$

Days Receivables/Sales Outstanding Ratio

Profit is the primary focal accounting figure. The most important factor for a business is that they receive the cash and profit for whatever sales they make, and only then can the business progress further. To calculate and analyze this, we use the following formula:

$$\text{DSO Ratio} = \frac{\text{Accounts Receivable}}{\text{Average Sales per Day}}$$

The need for this ratio is to clearly show how efficiently we are receiving profit based on the sales that we make on a daily basis. If you analyze FMCG companies, you will see that the return is usually within 5 days or a week. This is because the cash is received hand-to-hand and as soon as possible with minimal issues. Distributors pay companies up front, just as the average customer pays the retailer upfront. On the other hand, power and energy companies are one of those companies that receive cash after severe delays. It can take up to six months to receive the cash.

Debt Equity Ratio

If you receive money slowly from your customers or have instances where you do not receive cash at all, you will require funds to help keep your company afloat. The quicker you receive the cash, the faster you can reinvest to acquire fixed assets and pay your employees. You may come to a position where you need to borrow more money and acquire debt. You need to first differentiate and classify what is good debt and what is bad debt. Try to eliminate bad debt and then calculate the debt-equity ratio.

To calculate a debt-equity ratio, use the following formula:

$$\text{Debt/Equity Ratio} = \frac{\text{Total Liabilities}}{\text{Total Shareholder Equity}}$$

Planning

Before we start planning our financial future, we need to first carefully evaluate our current financial position. The previous step, which is the financial analysis step, is the one where you calculated what your financial standing is. The next step of an FP&A cycle for a company is financial planning.

The core of any financial planning is based on two key principles:

1. It should be simple to plan.
2. It should be simple to execute.

A great plan always starts with what your end goals are. Where you wish to see yourself financially, and how to achieve that is where we begin our planning.

Setting Goals

For every business to grow you need to set specific goals. While creating excellent products and providing great service is what drives growth, money needs to be one of the main points of focus as well.

1. **Increase Revenue** – To start by stating the obvious, you need to examine your company and see what are the best financial opportunities you can avail to make the most revenue possible.

Whether you need to increase sales, do more marketing, hike up prices, etc. Whatever goal you decide on, make sure it is worked upon as specifically as possible. Depending on your company, you need to get more and more specific.

2. **Decrease Costs** – The number one reason why new businesses fail is that they fail to address and control where their money is going and what the costs associated are concerning their expenses. Profit and loss are not calculated simply by the number of sales. It matters most how much less had to be spent to make the most money. Scrutinize and review your expenses to see if you can lower utility costs, lessen wastage, negotiate contracts for a better deal, lower interests, increase efficiency, etc.

3. **Cash Flow Planning** – Most business owners neglect how and where their money is being spent, and where it is coming from. You need to create a detailed cash flow statement to see the exact amount of money being allocated and spent each month to avoid future conflicts and potential halts in operations.

4. **Debt Elimination** – Evaluate the amount of debt you have, and if the debt is on interest, then calculate how much interest you are

paying and how much it increases in a specific time. You might need to assess your sources of financing (equity, debt, or others) to make sure your company's financing is optimal. Make sure to pay back your lenders as soon as possible to avoid snowballing into bankruptcy.

5. **Improve Your Margins** – One of the many ways to increase profit and revenue is by reducing costs and increasing profit margins. You can cut down on costs in manufacturing and increase the prices. A delicate test needs to be conducted before raising prices because you can lose sales if prices increase. Make sure not to increase prices to a point you cannot make enough sales and end up making less money than you were before.

Forecasting

Once the financial analysis and planning phase has been done, it is time to predict the future. Financial forecasting is the process of predicting the future performance of an organization. To forecast the financial health of an organization, historical data is utilized to predict the future revenues of the company. This helps the management to adequately allocate the budget for the different departments.

Forecasting is critical for the growth of a business. Investors usually utilize forecasts to analyze the future performance of the company before investing in its shares. This increases or decreases the share price of an organization. In addition to this, economists also determine the macro factors like GDP and unemployment rate by reviewing the financial forecasting of the companies.

Chapter 4 – Importance of Project Management Skills

When talking about projects in finance, one aspect that repeatedly comes up is that of financial management. This brings about the role of all the people involved in project management, particularly those called financial analysts. The chapter will discuss their role and potential in detail and their contribution to any organization or team. On a surface level, the primary role of a financial analyst boils down to accumulating and then scrutinizing data to evaluate outcomes for business decisions or investment recommendations.

There are varying posts for financial analysts in several organizations that range from junior most to senior-most capacities, and it is often a creative niche that creates other professional opportunities and is not limited. That was the gist of what financial analysts tend to do over the span of their professional lives. Now, let us delve into details about what financial analysts really do and how they are also financial planners for organizations.

If one was to dive into specifics, then it can be said that financial analysts study macroeconomic as well as microeconomic situations along with the basis and foundation of the company and its previous decisions to make their informed predictions about businesses and more. After their predictions, they also ensure to set out a course of action. This could include the likes of projecting the company's performance trends and growth opportunities and identifying areas to scale up or down as well as the overall outlook for the company. However, the financial analyst must keep the business interests in mind when making predictions or suggesting a course of action.

A financial expert should know about current advancements in the field in which they practice, just as in planning financial models to anticipate future monetary conditions for quite a few factors.

Not all financial analysts dissect the stock or security markets or help their bosses make speculations. Organizations may enlist an analyst to utilize mathematical information to pinpoint the viability of different advertising methods vis-a-vis costs, as an example.

Does this bring us to what truly constitutes a financial analyst? Of course, some skills will be discussed in detail over the course of this chapter. However, a few basics must be considered when looking at a financial analyst and the qualities that they need to have.

Contrasted with some lucrative skills, the capabilities to turn into a financial analyst are considerably less inflexible and clear-cut. In contrast to law and medication, no profession-wide educational essentials exist in the financial domain.

All things considered, in the 21st century, a four-year college education – ideally with a significance in financial aspects, money, or insights – has become an accepted prerequisite for turning into a financial investigator or analyst of any sort. Different majors that are viewed well incorporate accounting and math, and even science and designing — particularly if one has a premium in practicing as an examiner in those businesses. Certain educational degrees ranging from undergraduate and post-graduate levels can be required and need to be looked at as well.

Notwithstanding, an effective profession as a financial analyst requires solid quantitative abilities, mastered critical thinking capacities, adroitness in the utilization of rationale, or more normal relational abilities. Financial experts need to crunch information; however, they additionally need to report their discoveries to their bosses in an unmistakable, compact, and influential way.

As the chapter has progressed, it's becoming clearer what it takes to be a good financial analyst in a nutshell, but it is important to comprehend and understand that financial analysts, as argued earlier, are also financial planners. Therefore, it needs to be understood what a 'good and efficient financial analyst looks like. To make that clear, here are a few traits that need to be looked out for when looking for a financial analyst.

Leadership

The individuals who prevail in financial analysis are the individuals who are self-propelled and who can spur others to push ahead. Although you may not be applying to be a director or someone on an executive level and instead on a junior-level position, one requires a significant degree of authority capacities. Authority is the establishment upon which viable correspondence, collaboration, projection, and other day-by-day errands are based.

Leadership, in a nutshell, is the use of specific abilities, characteristics, and information to guarantee ideal execution and that the ideal outcomes are accomplished by individuals. How can financial analysts use leadership to become better at their jobs and lead projects more efficiently and make their respective organizations more successful? Here is a list of things that can be considered when looking for leadership skills in a financial analyst.

- Set up where outside help may be required
- Provide clear guidance and support correspondence
- Delegate duty fittingly and reasonably
- Think about expected obstructions or limitations
- Distinguish and comprehend the goal
- Trust others to utilize their judgment
- Settle on and execute choices
- Intercede when important
- Plan to accomplish the objective
- Show appreciation
- Screen progress
- Fulfill time constraints
- Give Criticism

As leaders, when financial analysts use these tactics, they tend to have motivated employees working under them and create an atmosphere of productivity and efficiency. This also allows for better work, and in turn, a better profitability rate for the company or organization involved. It would be a fair assumption to make if one said that a financial analyst's leadership qualities and abilities are critical to the progression, growth, and profitability of the company.

ROI Estimation

It is often said that time is money, particularly when there is a business and its profitability at stake. Incidentally, time and money both are aspects of business that are deeply connected with the company's financial planning and, therefore, are a part of financial project management. Here, cost and time assessment become integral, along with the return on the company's investment in a project. This is a task carried out by the financial analyst.

ROI assessment in a project is how to gauge the financial gain or loss of a project in relation to its expected cost in order to finish an undertaking within a characterized scope. ROI assessment represents every component needed for the venture - from materials to labor and assessing an aggregate sum that decides an undertaking's financial plan. ROI helps decide if a company should undertake the project. If the ROI comes in too low, a company may choose to pare down the undertaking to focus on other projects with better ROI or otherwise use the company's funds more effectively.

Ability to Delegate

Delegation is important for many reasons when it comes to project management, particularly in finance. Analysts must delegate work when required to make sure they are not overworked or make mistakes. More so, everyone has different specializations. For example, someone might have a better understanding of working with a particular industry, and if they do, it is best to delegate. How can financial analysts delegate in organizations? Here is a checklist that can be followed.

- Keep a delegation disposition. Ask yourself often: "Who else could do this?" Question each assignment, especially those you have accomplished for quite a long time.

- Characterize the ideal result. Ask: "What is the outcome I need to achieve?" Learn to appoint duty regarding accomplishing results instead of dumping errands.

- Select the individual. Think about more than one standard when deciding to whom to appoint something. A few interesting points: Who has insight and abilities? (Be mindful so as not to over-burden this individual.) Who needs to figure out how to deal with this obligation? Who has the opportunity to acknowledge this obligation? Who might want to have this chance?

- Get contributions from others. Request thoughts regarding what to change, whom to include, and how to characterize the outcomes.

- Relegate the duty and characterize the time factors. What is the cutoff time? When will you need progress reports?

- Give preparing direction. Does the individual need to prepare before accepting this accountability? What direction will they have to succeed? Make sure to permit them opportunities for autonomous reasoning.

- Characterize the position level. How much force will they require? What sorts of force? Who else has to realize that this individual has the power to act? Make certain to illuminate them to guarantee participation with the representative.

- Concur about the control interaction. What sorts of controls are required? How might one feel in charge and still engage representatives to act freely?

- Screen progress. Focus and keep up control of the circumstance. Administrators are as yet liable for the achievement or disappointment of this individual and for accomplishing the ideal outcomes.

- Give criticism. Keep in contact, giving a lot of encouraging feedback, and instructing when required.

- Distinguish the exercises learned. What did the representative realize? What did you realize? The individual with the new obligation will frequently sort out better approaches to complete things, and such enhancements should be distinguished, recorded, and shared.

- Assess execution. Give the individual accommodating input. What did they progress admirably? Where would they be able to improve? How might the outcomes be improved? How could the chief make a superior showing of aiding them to succeed?

Communication Skills

Financial analysts should also possess communication skills, as these skills can directly influence interpersonal relations. Effective communication as a financial analyst can mean being direct when sending emails, leaving phone messages, speaking to an investor about important financial information, and utilizing nonverbal communication to navigating professional and working relationships.

Communication is key for any and every management position; however, it becomes even more important when this communication has to do with the amount of money going in and then coming back into the company. Even if there is a lapse of communication for one transaction or one prediction, all financial projects will find themselves in utter chaos. Moreover, it could cause the company a significant number of losses, which no company would be looking to entertain.

Research-Based Data Analysis

Over the years, with the advent of big data, storage and access to data have become easy, and every aspect of project management has had to rely heavily upon research-based data to make decisions.

The thing remains that the demand for analytics-driven decision-making across the business has continuously increased. As more departments build analytic capabilities, finance analytics governance becomes unclear. What role should finance analytics play for the company? How do the best finance teams support analytics?

The answer remains rather simple here. The financial analysts need to work together based on data that has come their way in the past and is about to come their way as well. They must know of the kind of capital put into the business from the very first day to the kind of money going out and profit coming into the business until the very hour they begin their analysis and decision-making.

This would help them make better predictions, and better predictions ultimately lead to better decisions, leading to a growing and successful organization. Doesn't that fulfill the very purpose of project management? It does! Working well with data and making informed decisions while keeping all research in mind is also something that allows for better financial navigation, be it for short or long-term management.

More so, data and research keep an organization ahead of its competitors. It ensures that their organization does not take the financial decisions that went against a particular competitor, and that remains just one of the many reasons why data and research-based choices need to come from financial analysts. It also provides historic evidence and proof of failed or successful business decisions, which help the existing organization progress in the best possible way and allow the financial analyst to progress.

Financial Analyst and Cross-functional Stakeholders

Financial analysts are one of only a handful few capacities that associate and collaborate with cross-functional groups across the company as a piece of the customary workday. Most FP&A groups are separated into focal groups and decentralized assets inserted into the different offices they support.

Focal FP&A groups are engaged with amassing and examining organization-level execution and patterns. They drive cycles like yearly financial plans, figures, capital arranging, business blend examination, streamlining appraisals, and so on, which require joining forces with different capacities across the association at various stages just as senior partners like the CEO, CFO and Marketing Director.

Decentralized inserted FP&A analyst-based assets fill in as business accomplices to the groups they are planned to like promoting inventory network, R&D, sourcing, and so forth. They also work intimately with the individual business groups on arrangement, investigation, and business choice help. For instance, a Brand Financial Analyst in a Consumer Products organization like Procter and Gamble is a basic piece of a Brand Marketing group. He would accomplice consistently with the Brand Manager for building conjectures, arranging showcasing spends, performing an examination, for example, rivalry following, and so forth.

In numerous occurrences, FP&A professionals are aligned with the duty of heading cross-functional ventures, for example cost streamlining undertakings or advancement of financial dashboards. Furthermore, FP&A groups consistently work with IT in mechanizing or improving their processes.

Such cross-functional nature of work helps FP&A professionals foster comprehension of the measurements, inspirations, points of view, and subtleties of different capacities.

Cross-functional Moves

While the times have caused developments inside finance to appear dreary, they have also opened up new freedoms for FP&A professionals who have progressively experienced better business inclusion and an extended business range of abilities past conventional roles. It's anything but an uncommon sight these days to see an FP&A professional proceeding to expect jobs outside finance, such as project management, data & analytics, or business development with incredible achievement.

There have been cases where a Brand Financial Analyst in a Consumer Products organization proceeded onward to turn into a Brand Manager and is presently heading a whole item class. This individual acquired an exhaustive comprehension of Brand Marketing with its obligations and subtleties during his Brand Finance stretch. At a certain point, he realized the brand's portions of the overall industry and portion of voice in media better than the Brand director himself; given the examination, he was continually racing to recognize systems for the brand to develop. This puts him in a brilliant position to request this development, and the association was additionally open to entrusting him with it.

Another such case is of a financial investigator supporting the store network vertical of a significant online business player. Through his business joining forces and investigation of transportation and warehousing cost improvement, he had the option to foster an extremely careful comprehension of the production network as a capacity. What he lacked in terms of education, in-store network, the executives or activities, he compensated for with his unrivaled insightful and versatile capacities while likewise getting on the functional subtleties at work.

Business Analytics: An Opportunity or Threat?

Other than the cross-functional developments into the divisions one is installed into, a fascinating chance exists in Business Analytics. The investigation is the popular expression of the decade, and associations across areas and topographies are intensely setting up Analytics groups.

At present, most Analytics groups are being set up under the Technology divisions. FP&A professionals ought to, as I would like to think, see this as a chance just as an expected existential danger. These analytics groups are investigating large information and recognizing patterns and bits of knowledge for the business. FP&A groups have been doing likewise work for quite a long time, but with a financial core interest. It is just consistent that FP&A heads likewise head Business Analytics divisions.

Taking everything into account, fascinating vocation ways are arising for FP&A professionals and will progressively lead them out of finance domain limits. In our current reality, where specialization is everything, core business information and capacity stay the most crucial expertise that a business chief requires. A proficient FP&A analyst is intently mindful of business patterns, and bits of knowledge work with cross-functional groups to impact better dynamics and is fundamentally an in-house expert of sorts. Moving up to genuine business dynamic jobs has its difficulties yet is conceivable and getting more typical.

Financial analysis is the backbone of any program or project. If the finances are taken care of in the best possible way, most things can be cared for. In fact, most decisions depend on the financial feasibility of the decision, which comes down to the important tasks FP&A professionals play. Therefore, it is absolutely integral to have an efficient and competent financial analyst!

Chapter 5 – The Salary Guide

The world of business has become more and more competitive over time. With so many entrants coming in every day, it is tough for businesses to maintain their profitability, and maintain an edge over their competitors. Moreover, the COVID-19 pandemic has made things a lot more difficult than necessary. In these trying times, the role of FP&A professionals in an organization has become even more crucial.

Contrary to popular belief, the role of an FP&A professional is quite different from that of an investment banker or a consultant. With a connotation of uniqueness attached to it, the field of FP&A is extremely mouthwatering for fresh graduates and younger professionals, trying to make it big on the professional front.

While some are excited, there is still a fair amount of skepticism that exists. A fair majority of newbies aren't sure whether or not they should pursue a career in FP&A. If you fall into the latter category, this chapter is strictly for you. In this chapter, I will take you through the entire career hierarchy of the people who opt for this field of work. Also, I will discuss the salary structure that exists at the moment, and how it changes throughout this career path. However, before we move forth, let's take a minute to shed some light on all the activities an FP&A professional is involved in.

What Do FP&A Professionals Do?

Simply put. FP&A is an in-house financial role in the corporate world. Over time, these FP&A analysts and managers provide information and analysis to the senior management of a business before they make important financial decisions. These people are also responsible for running the forecasting and budgeting process, as well as looking after the cash flow forecast models. They also take care of the variance models and some other financial performance tools. This department works closely with the treasury and shares ideas on cash flows and expenditures.

The FP&A Career Path

Usually, the career path for an FP&A professional start from the point where he graduates from college, usually with a degree in business or finance. From there, either the individual might go to a Fortune 500 company in the accounts and finance department, work for a bank, or he would spend a couple of years in public accounting. From there, he gets in a good position where he can easily land a job as an FP&A analyst. In parallel, he or she can pursue an MBA in the relevant field. From an analyst, he can graduate to the position of a senior analyst, and then he can culminate his career as a manager or a director, and so on.

Now that we have an overview, let's delve deeper. In the following paragraphs, we will take a look at all the different positions an FP&A professional will occupy throughout his career in the field. Moreover, we will take a look at all the things they will be responsible for, as well as the salary packages they will be offered at each stage.

FP&A Analyst

As I have already discussed in the previous sections, an FP&A analyst is in the beginning stage. It sounds funny, but an analyst is the workhorse of the FP&A hierarchy. Their job description includes the following responsibilities.

- Gathering data
- Building and maintaining models
- Coordinating across various circles

The salary[2] range for an analyst starts at $60k and goes all the way to $75k. Before an individual makes it to the analyst stage, he has already had an undergraduate degree. In this role, often companies hire a fresh graduate out of college.

FP&A Associate

The job of a senior analyst apart from directing the junior analysts is to run models, as well as run the financial modeling process. The salary range[3] for a senior analyst starts from $85k and ends at somewhere around $95k. To be hired as an FP&A associate, one needs to have a bachelor's degree and several years of experience as an Analyst of at least 3-5 years in the field of finance or have a master's degree such as an MBA.

---

2 Financial Planning & Analysis (FP&A) Overview. (n.d.). Corporate Finance Institute. https://corporatefinanceinstitute.com/resources/careers/map/corporate/fpa-analyst-career/

3 FP&A salaries. (n.d.). Abacum. https://www.abacum.io/blog/the-2021-guide-to-fpa-salaries

FP&A Manager

After a person has worked as an Associate or a Senior Associate for a few years, he possesses the experience and the skills that are needed to fit into a managerial position. As a manager, he can serve as an individual contributor in the planning cycle. As far as the salary range[4] is concerned, an FP&A manager makes somewhere between $115k to $130k. To occupy the manager's role, you need an MBA degree from a reputable institution, combined with at least 5 to 10 years of proven experience in FP&A.

Director/ Vice President of FP&A

The director or the VP is responsible for looking after the work-related activities of managers and the analysts that work closely with them. If we look at their salary bracket, it starts at somewhere around $150k and goes all the way to $225k which includes stock options and bonuses. To qualify for this role, one needs to have work experience of at least 10 years. The person who qualifies for this position has already run several years of corporate FP&A planning, budgeting, and forecasting cycles, as well as implemented new processes, and has led different projects.

---

4 FP&A Career Path. (n.d.). Wall Street Prep. https://www.wallstreetprep.com/knowledge/fpa-career-path-salary-guide-analyst-director/

What's Next?

Up until now, we have discussed the four main positions within the FP&A hierarchy, their responsibilities, their salary brackets, as well as the experience they need to qualify for their respective position. But what happens, after a person has made it past the VP/director stage? Let's find out.

After they have made it to the VP/director stage, most FP&A professionals tend to stay there. However, some of them seek similar positions in other organizations, depending on whether they are offered a better package. In bigger organizations, VPs and directors choose to stay with their companies, while progressing internally and taking care of relatively bigger P&Ls.

There is also a possibility of being promoted to the position of CFO, but because there is only one position, the competition is very tough. However, if a professional chooses to stick around long enough, their likelihood of being promoted to the position of the CFO is high, unless the company decides to bring someone from the outside, which happens often. However, if the individual rotates to other departments such as business development, corporate development, operations, and control, they can further their portfolio to qualify for the position of CFO.

There is another possibility, and that is to become the CEO, but again, there is only one position and the competition is high. Then some don't want to spend any more time in the hopes of making it to the top. These individuals bid farewell to their careers in financial planning and analysis and take the entrepreneurial route. They go forth and use their experience in the corporate world to set up their businesses across a variety of industries.

FP&A for People with Non-Traditional Profiles

As I have already talked about, the entry points for an FP&A can vary from one candidate to another. While some candidates enter simultaneously as they're pursuing their degrees, others tend to enter after they are done with their MBAs. Although it is better to make an early entry, here are some ways for late entrants to work their way up the hierarchy, and improve their professional profile within the field.

Applicants for the Position of a Junior Analyst

Let's suppose you are applying for a beginner-level position, but you don't have former experience in the field of accounting and finance. Not a problem. Some people might tell you that you won't make it, but the truth is, you can be quite successful if you play your cards right. There are a couple of designations you can earn which will help you as you go forth. For example, a CPA or a CFA would be extremely effective. You can even get a hold of an FP&A designation from the Association of Financial Professionals. Some people switch from investment banking, but that doesn't happen very often. However, the experience that you receive in investment banking always tends to work in your favor as it closely relates to working with financial models, if you are willing to do something in FP&A.

Applicants for Managerial Positions in FP&A

If you are looking for a more senior role such as that of a manager, it is going to be a little tough. In order to get hired as a senior resource in this field, first of all, you will need an MBA degree with a specialization in Accounting and Finance. On top of that, you will be needing significant experience in the industry where you managed different projects, as well as corporate initiatives. Transitioning from being a generalist or a healthcare person to a senior-level FP&A professional is next to impossible.

Work-Life Balance

It sounds a little strange, but in reality, an FP&A professional can maintain a better work-life balance, compared to people working in investment banking or some form of consulting. An FP&A professional works somewhere 45 to 50 hours a week. However, during fire drills and in the peak seasons such as budgets, the number of hours can go up to 60 or 70 hours in a week. In public companies, FP&A teams tend to work a little harder than other companies, especially during the quarterly financial close period. The workload during this period is high, and there are times when people work up to 80 hours in those weeks.

What to Expect?

Let's suppose, you have just landed an interview for the position of an FP&A professional. What you need is a thorough knowledge of both behavioral as well as technical questions. While behavioral questions can be easy to answer, it requires a bit of preparation and thinking through your previous experience to answer situation-specific questions. The technical questions are aimed strictly at financial analysis, financial modeling, and accounting. During the interview, you can always expect questions similar to the ones mentioned below.

- How will you come up with a financial model?
- How can we evaluate the financial performance of our business?

Reasons to Work in FP&A

To be honest, working in the field of FP&A is very exciting. The professional responsible for these roles play an important role in financial modeling for executive decision-making, which in a way is the life and blood of any business. These individuals tend to work closely with the CFO of the company and they play a vital role in decisions related to capital spending, operating budgets, as well as long-term financial planning.

This department is also needed when there are mergers or acquisitions taking place. If you can make it, the FP&A department is a safe place to work. This department is needed in good and bad times, and the good thing is that it always tends to allow you to learn and grow. Also, there are too many fluctuations, and the department mostly remains stable. Here are some of the things an FP&A professional is responsible for, though it varies by the industry and specific role they're working in:

- Performing and presenting the quantitative analysis of the operational and financial data

- Building and maintaining financial databases by analyzing and organizing a big range of data sources

- Coming up with a financial report for use within the company by collecting, sorting, and formatting information

- The evaluation of different investment opportunities by comparing them with one another

- Appraising the current condition of the company's assets, as well as the use life, and also evaluating them

- Recommendations regarding financing structures, and considerations regarding the company's cost of capital

- Coming up with budgets, as well as a comprehensive forecast about the performance of the business in the future

- Building and maintaining a full-fledged financial model, that provides a detail of the company's current operations, as well as projections regarding the future performance of the business

- Performing ad hoc analysis for executives, whenever needed

Chapter 6 - Having To Be Assigned The 'Special Projects

As an FP&A professional, you will find yourself working on some special projects either quite frequently. The scope of such projects varies from organization to organization. However, the following points are considered by FP&A professionals while working on special projects.

1. Market Reach and Research
2. Optimization Of Process
3. Identifying Potential Targets
4. Allocation Of Capital

Let's discuss the above points in detail for a better understanding of readers.

Market Research

FP&A professionals working on projects need to create business cases for the same, and the investment needed. For this reason, Market research is the starting point. Market research is described as the process of determining the viability of a new product or service, or new system by conducting research. This strategy enables firms or organizations to identify their target market, collect and document feedback, and make educated decisions. Market research can be carried out in-house by organizations or enterprises, or it can be outsourced to firms with experience in the field. Surveys, product testing, and focus groups can all be used to accomplish this. For their time, test subjects are frequently provided with product samples or a small stipend. Market research is an integral part of a new product or service's research and development, and FP&A plays a critical role in assessing the financials here.

The primary goal of market research is to comprehend or evaluate the market for a specific product or service to predict how the target audience will react to it. Market research information can be used to modify marketing/advertising operations or to discover what features consumers value most and what services they desire.

There are two types of market research. They are as follows.

    a. **Primary Research**

    b. **Secondary Research**

Now, I will discuss both types in detail.

Primary Research

The data that the corporation has obtained directly or that has been collected by a person or organization engaged to do the study is referred to as primary research. There are two types of research in this category: exploratory and specific research.

Exploratory research is a less structured option and functions via more open-ended questions, and it results in questions or issues being presented that the company may need to address. Specific research, on the other hand, finds answers to previously identified issues that are often brought to attention through exploratory research.[5]

Primary research is a combination of qualitative and quantitative research. Therefore, the methods used to conduct this type of research include the following processes

---

5 Alexandra Twin (2021), Market Research, Investopedia, Retrieved From: https://www.investopedia.com/terms/m/market-research.asp

i. One-On-One Interviews

As the name implies, this method entails personal interaction in the form of an interview, in which the researcher asks the respondents a series of questions to collect information or data. The questions are mainly open-ended and written in a way that encourages responses. This strategy is highly reliant on the interviewer's ability and expertise in asking questions that elicit responses.

ii. Focus Group

One of the most common qualitative research methodologies is the focus group. A focus group is a small group of persons (6-10) who are often asked to participate in online surveys. The nicest part of focus groups is that the data can be obtained remotely without having to engage with the group members individually. However, because it is used to acquire complicated data, this method is more expensive.

Secondary Research

Secondary research makes use of data compiled by third parties such as government organizations, the media, and chambers of business. Newspapers, periodicals, books, commercial websites, free government, and nongovernment institutions. The following sources are utilized for secondary research.

i. Public Sources

Public sources, such as libraries, are fantastic places to find free information. Government libraries usually provide free services, and a researcher can chronicle the available material.

ii. Commercial Sources

Commercial sources, while reliable, are costly. Commercial sources of information include local newspapers, magazines, journals, and television.

iii. Educational Sources

Although not a popular source of information, most universities and educational institutions are significant sources of data because they conduct more research projects than any other industry.

The FP&A professionals conduct market research to determine the size of the potential market so that they can plan and forecast the financial probabilities accordingly.

Optimization Of Process

Process optimization is the art of fine-tuning a process to optimize a set of parameters while adhering to a few limitations. The most common objectives are to reduce costs while increasing efficiency. One of the most important quantitative instruments in industrial decision-making is process optimization.

Workflow inefficiency emerges when diverse technical systems and tools don't "talk to one other," which is a persistent challenge for large enterprises. This frequently necessitates time-consuming manual intervention. Because FP&A teams are often at the center of inefficient processes, they are commonly tasked with fixing them.

It is critical to be aware of potential stumbling blocks to successfully move process optimization ahead. This involves accounting for the time-consuming budgeting and planning process, which necessitates the integration of financial and operational data. It's crucial to comprehend the vital role that a centralized corporate performance management strategy plays in those procedures. This shift in perspective makes room for change. As a result, the goal is "democratization" of planning, which means that all essential stakeholders play an essential part in moving the company toward process optimization.

Identifying Potential Targets (Mergers and Acquisitions)

Another vital part of the FP&A specialist's task can be to identify potential acquisitions that the organization can acquire quickly and efficiently. Though this is more commonly part of corporate strategy functions in many organizations, some FP&A professionals in different companies are also leading this effort.

Going for suitable mergers and acquiring profitable ventures can result in a company's exponential growth. FP&A professionals take these steps for mergers and acquisitions.

Get Involved in The Early Stages

The FP&A professionals get involved in the early stages of the mergers and acquisitions process. They gather all necessary information about a potential target, forecast its future, and advise the organization to acquire or leave the acquisition.

Rely On Past Experience

The FP&A specialists rely on their past experiences as well to analyze whether a company can manage an acquisition or merger efficiently. This helps them in finalizing their decisions.

Review Transition Cost Estimates

The FP&A professionals review the transitional costs and expected revenues that they foresee a company would generate. This analysis is a crucial part of the M&A process, and almost the whole process relies on this analysis.

Ensuring Information Is Unbiased

The FP&A professionals ensure that the information they have gathered is unbiased and free of concoctions. It helps them in conducting their reviews properly.

Allocation Of Capital

Capital allocation is the process through which a company determines where and how to spend the money it has earned. Capital allocation refers to how a company's financial resources are distributed and invested to boost efficiency and profits. The goal of a company's management is to distribute capital in such a way that it generates the most wealth for its owners as possible. Allocating capital is difficult, and capital allocation decisions often determine whether a company succeeds or fails. Management must examine the viability of the various investment alternatives, assess each one's possible consequences on the company, and deploy the additional funds effectively and in a manner that will create the best overall results for the company.

FP&A specialists guide organizations in the allocation of their capital in the most beneficial ways. As we all know that the goal of an FP&A specialist is to maximize a company's revenue and forecast its financial future by utilizing statistical tools and charts. They utilize their statistical knowledge in the allocation of capital as well. The following approaches are used by FP&A specialists in the allocation of capital.

Strategic Capital Budgeting

The first step in capital allocation is strategic capital budgeting. It is a conventional FP&A approach for the allocation of capital. What they do is that they invest in companies rather than projects, convert portfolio roles into capital allocation criteria, and strive for well-balanced portfolios.

Invest In Businesses Rather Than Projects

It's all about looking at the forest and the trees when it comes to capital allocation, and top performers prioritize the forest. Outperformers in capital allocation invest systematically in businesses that add value both strategically and financially, whereas underperformers invest excessively in value-depleting expansion.

Assign Portfolio Roles into Capital Allocation Guidelines

A smart strategy to link strategic potential to resource allocation is to assign specific roles to the individual firms in the portfolio and set appropriate capital allocation standards.

Balancing The Investment Portfolio

Analyzing a company's investment program from a portfolio viewpoint is another technique to link corporate strategy to capital allocation. So, basically, by utilizing this technique, the FP&A specialists divert the invested funds from one project to another to balance out the overall investment portfolio keeping in mind overall company's long term strategy and vision.

Investment Project Selection

Outperformers ensure that they completely grasp the financial profile of the projects in question, the quality of the forecasts, the variability of cash flows, and the payback profile over time when determining to fund particular capital projects.

Think Out of The Box; Go Beyond Internal Rate of Return (IRR)

In theory, choosing among competing investment projects is as simple as sorting the list by predicted internal rate of return and selecting the projects with the highest IRRs until the capital is fully committed. However, in practice, the efficiency of this strategy is limited by the validity of the assumptions used in valuations and the influence of other criteria that are not apparent in selection judgments.

Requiring all business cases for big investment projects to include a model that highlights the essential business drivers is an excellent method to improve the quality of assumptions. This clarifies essential assumptions and allows decision-makers to comprehend the influence of key drivers. It also makes simple sensitivity and scenario evaluations easier. Managers can compute the crucial variable breakeven points that must be met for the project to create value.

Chapter 7 – Benefits and Limitations of Financial Planning & Analysis

An organization needs to have an FP&A department at its disposal. If not for the financial planning for an organization, things are bound to go south rather quickly. As a result, many financial statements come into the picture. Financial statements are financial information records an organization distributes yearly, half-yearly, quarterly, or on a month-to-month premise. These archives incorporate the organization's total assets dependent on resources and liabilities, just as the organization's costs, income, and operational spending plan. Financial organizers, senior leaders, and bookkeepers may utilize financial statements to settle on future planning, developments, and item dispatches; however, there are drawbacks to using this technique and financial planning and analysis in general.

Let us take a look at the benefits first.

The Ability to Detect Patterns

FP&A professionals uncover how much an organization procures each year in sales and the potential for the organization. The agreements may vacillate, yet financial organizers ought to have the option to recognize an example over long periods of marketing projections. For instance, the organization may have an example of expanded sales when another item is delivered. The sales may drop following a year or so of being available. This is useful, as it shows potential and sales designs, so chiefs know to anticipate a drop in sales.

A Chance to Budget Outline

Another benefit of analyzing financial statements for dynamic future planning is that they show spending plans. The financial goals uncover how much leeway the organization needs to spend on dispatching items, creating showcasing efforts, growing the current office size, etc. Realizing how much money is accessible for dynamic planning guarantees that the organization doesn't spend more than anticipated.

Cash Flow and Income Review

An income statement and a cash flow statement are key financial statements utilized in economic analysis. As the name suggests, a cash flow statement represents money in and money out. You can think of it as a checking account of a company where deposits are cash inflows while withdrawals are cash outflows, and it shows the financial dissolvability of an organization to pay its liabilities at any given time. A few organizations have repeating incomes yet ongoing costs. As an example, realizing that a sluggish previous quarter of costs is needed to support the Christmas surge is significant for business proprietors to oversee his financial assets. It isn't just that but the general understanding of what is going in, what is going out, and what is expected in the future on the same front.

Organization Liability Review

The financial analysis put forth the situation of the current liabilities as well as the ones expected in the future. These incorporate business advances, credit extensions, charge cards, and credit stretched out from sellers. A business proprietor who intends to apply for a business extension credit can take a gander at the financial statements and decide whether he needs to decrease existing liabilities before applying. Banks take a gander at the financial statements and think about the incomes, assets, and existing liabilities.

Audit Assets and Inventory

The monetary record is a part of the financial statement and planning. Assets are remembered for their economic history. Breaking down whether there is excessive stock or too little aids business proprietors get ready for impending deals. Keeping a lot of inventory available is a potential issue that ties up money, while not having sufficient stock can prompt losing clients and a portion of the overall industry.

Distinguish Trends and Determine Steps Needed

Examining the financial statements and analyzing them from one quarter to another and year to year help business proprietors see patterns in development. A youthful business may have misfortunes in the early years while creating items and a client base. Simultaneously, statements show whether the business proprietor is meeting projected appraisals.

If a business is projecting a 10% yearly development yet just accomplishing 7%, business pioneers need to search for approaches to reduce expenses or increase incomes.

Looking for Investment Capital

When a business looks for accomplices or financial backers, the financial statements and the plans made for the future are basic fodder for the investor. Investigating the reports not just assists financial backers with deciding whether an organization is bringing in money, yet it likewise helps with recognizing a sensible cost for every offer. Investors typically put capital in a development organization; along these lines, investor value is characterized as dependent on the capital investment added to assets, with liabilities deducted to represent total investor value.

For instance, if an organization has $1 million in assets with $500,000 in liabilities and gets another $500,000 in investment capital, the all-out investor value is $1 million ($1,000,000 assets + $500,000 investment - $500,000 liabilities = $1,000,000).

Smart Budget Allocation

This is closely related to cash flow management and cost reductions. Once you have a clear understanding of the amount of funding you have to spend - whether through sales income or investments - you need to figure out how you'll finish it. The company has its overall budget - essentially its "burn rate" for each quarter or year. Break this down into specific team budgets (product development, marketing, customer support, etc.), and ensure that the amounts dedicated to each reflect their importance.

Budgets give each team their constraints from within which to build. They know what resources are available to them and plan out campaigns and personal or product development accordingly. At the company level, tracking project or team budgets will always be more manageable than monitoring spending as a whole. Once you break each budget down, it's relatively straightforward to keep an eye on who's spending what.

Necessary Cost Reductions

Aside from setting out how much you can afford to spend (and on what), a financial plan also lets you spot savings ahead of time. If you've already been in business for some time, building your financial plan involves first looking back at what you've already spent and how fast you're currently growing. As you set out your budget(s) for next year, you'll refer back to past spending and identify unnecessary or over-inflated costs along the way. And then, for next year's budget, you adjust accordingly.

This conscious effort is all part of spending control, the practice of keeping company spending in line with your expectations. Even better, a quarterly or annual review almost always unearths areas where you can save money and put your resources to better use.

Risk mitigation

A crucial aspect of the finance team's role is to help companies avoid and navigate risk - from financial fraud to economic crisis. And while plenty of chances are hard to predict or even avoid, there are plenty that you can see coming.

Your financial plan should make room for certain business insurance expenses, and losses through risky inefficiencies and perhaps set aside resources for unexpected costs. Particularly during turbulent times, you may create several financial forecasts that show different outcomes for the business: one where revenue is easy to come by and one or two others where times are more challenging.

Again, the point is to have contingency plans in place and to attempt to determine how your roadmap changes if you grow only 20% next quarter instead of 30% (or 50%). There's no reason to go overboard, but you can find risky areas within the business and consider your best responses if things go wrong.

Crisis management

The first thing that tends to happen in any company crisis is your review and rebuild your plans. This, of course, means that you must have a clear business plan in the first place. Otherwise, your crisis response is to improvise. At the time of writing this book, as the 2020 financial crisis unfolds, the critical refrain we've heard from finance leaders is the need to forecast constantly. Nobody truly knows when the crisis will end or how it will have impacted their business. So, companies are creating new financial plans on a monthly or quarterly basis, at least.

And those with robust and well-thought-out financial plans will find this process easier. They're not starting from scratch over and over, and they've already identified apparent risks and the key levers to pull in response.

It Acts as a Development Guide

At last, your financial arrangement assists you with dissecting your present circumstances and project where you need the business to be later on. Once more, your more extensive business plan will do this on a comprehensive level: the business sectors you'd prefer to be in, the number of workers you'll have, and the items or administrations you desire to sell.

The financial area adds information to these objectives and plugs in your degree of investment en route. For instance, on the off chance that you wish to enlist 100 new workers this year, your financial arrangement will probably have to incorporate enrollment specialists and a particular spending plan to discover a unique ability.

Set aside the effort to set out how huge you anticipate that the company should be, your costs with a more prominent organization, and the measure of income coming in to redress. On the off chance that you've raised investment to help develop financially, you can presumably hope to consume cash quicker than you make it - this is ordinary.

However, assuming you consume money and can't arrive at your development targets, you'll need to rethink your position. So set those development focuses out now, and you'll have the option to survey as you go.

The straightforwardness with Normal Staff and Finance Staff

I previously referenced how vital your financial arrangement is for financial leaders, so I will not plunge into them more here. Be that as it may, the equivalent is valid for staff. It is presently expected that organization leaders will be transparent with the team. A few new businesses venture to such an extreme to plug their pay rates for the world to see.

In any event, current representatives need to see that the organization is in good hands and headed for progress. Furthermore, when chiefs can share the financial arrangement in gatherings required for everyone, they carry genuine information about what exactly would somehow or another be a business plan ailing in subtleties.

The role of an FP&A expert is to give exact, timely financial analysis and guidance to the heads of the association. While that sounds expansive and minimal more than calculating, the job brings substantially more worth than that. Indeed, recently FP&A has gone to the front as a vital and applicable benefit to associations, especially given the incredible speed at which organizations move today and the intricacy of the business climate. Several other intertwined benefits need to be looked at as well.

Performing financial planning is fundamental to the accomplishment of any business. It upholds the business plan and presents a cycle to guarantee the goals set are reachable according to a financial perspective. Adequate financial planning and analysis comprehend how well you project your business will do and gauges your prosperity compared with that projection. The interaction is progressing and should fill in as an intelligent manual for maintaining your business.

Besides, if subsidizing or financing is required, the FP&A work sets you up to introduce the financial segment of your business plan is generally a short request. Regardless of whether you are looking for investment from private value firms, financial speculators, or private investors, they will need to consider numbers to be proof that your business will develop and that there is an exit system for them not too far off, during which they can make a benefit. Any bank will request to see these numbers, too, to guarantee credit reimbursement.

Generally significant; nonetheless, you could say the FP&A work gets where accounting leaves off. While a regulator considers and records chronicled results, the FP&A work is future-centered. It connects the system to a long-range plan and yearly working and capital financial plans. It gives a multi-year economic demonstration and yearly objective setting measures. It utilizes the interaction of deciphering the essential focuses into thorough yearly working and capital financial plans. Also, it leads and administers the financial administration capacity to guarantee the conveyance of yearly spending results and reinforce income consistency.

Besides, consistency is significant, and a solid FP&A measure disposes of variety and welcomes predictable and dependable data on which to base level-headed and better choices. Furthermore, a very experienced FP&A expert or office will create and disseminate exemption reports, feature reports, and other scientific reports (i.e., proportion analysis) to upgrade the dynamic of the association's leadership.

CFO magazine expounded on the requirement for upgrades in FP&A 20 years prior, clarifying that altogether *"to be pertinent chasing after essential targets, finance groups needed to become more grounded business accomplices and create investigations that help chiefs increment monetary benefit."* It's a clarion call that reverberates today.

A solid FP&A capacity can be an agile, vital supporter of your association's prosperity, positively affecting its primary concern. However, specific weaknesses also need to be looked at in the process. Much like every other aspect of business and running an organization, FP&A, too, has some weaknesses. It's time to dive a bit into those now.

Based on Market Patterns

One detriment of utilizing financial statements is that the information and figures depend on availability at that given time. Contingent upon the market which might change rapidly; some leaders ought not to expect that the numbers from a past financial statement will continue as before or increment. Since an organization has sold 5 million duplicates of an item during one year doesn't promise it will sell a similar sum or more. It might sell significantly less if a contender delivers a comparable item.

At-One-Time Analysis

Another weakness is that a solitary financial statement shows how an organization is getting along at one single time. The financial information or analysis doesn't necessarily indicate whether the organization is improving or more regrettable than the prior year. On the off chance that leaders choose to utilize financial statements for settling on choices about the future, they should use a few financial statements from earlier months and years to guarantee they get a general image of how the organization is doing. The financial information turns into a ceaseless analysis, which is more helpful than utilizing a solitary statement.

Forecasting:

Financial plans are prepared by taking into account everyday situations in the future. Since the future is always uncertain and things may not happen as expected, the utility of financial planning is limited. The reliability of financial planning is debatable and very much doubted.

Changes:

Once a financial plan is prepared, then it becomes difficult to change it. A changed situation may demand a change in the financial plan, but managerial personnel may not like it. Even otherwise, assets might have been purchased, and raw material and labor costs might have been incurred. It becomes challenging to change a financial plan under such situations.

A Problem of Coordination:

The financial function is the most important of all the parts. Other processes influence a decision about the financial plan. While estimating financial needs, production policy, personnel requirements, and marketing possibilities are all taken into account. Unless there is a proper-coordination among all the functions, the preparation of a financial plan becomes difficult. Often there is a lack of coordination among different positions. Even indecision among personnel disturbs the process of financial planning.

Rapid Changes:

The growing mechanization of the industry is bringing rapid changes in the industrial process. The methods of production, marketing devices, consumer preferences, etc. create new demands every time. The incorporation of recent changes requires a shift in the financial plan every time.

Once investments are made in fixed assets, then these decisions cannot be reversed. It becomes complicated to adjust a financial plan for incorporating fast-changing situations. Unless a financial plan helps the adoption of new techniques, its utility becomes limited.

External and Miscellaneous Factors:

Outer elements that are not straightforwardly partners of your business plan yet may influence your planning antagonistically; for instance, war, cataclysmic events, and so on are amazingly troublesome and/or are difficult to anticipate. To beat these sorts of impediments, you ought to incorporate legitimate advances like protection to keep away from the misfortune that emerges because of these sorts of issues.

Time Consuming and Expensive Process:

Financial planning is a time-devouring action. It also requires the utilization of new advances and skills of various specialists, making this cycle costly. More often than not, businesses would prefer not to put a lot of resources into planning or don't have that much time to design appropriately, which may prompt off-base and poor planning. This limit can be overwhelmed by separating the venture into stages and afterward planning for each step independently.

However, the advantages of financial planning outnumber its limitations, and it is also important to note that even these limitations can be taken care of and overcome with efficient mitigation strategies and commitment to financial planning. The following listed ways can help overcome the limitations of FP&A.

- The planner should be given sufficient time and tools.

- Gather information and data from a very reliable source. The base data should be cross-checked with other sources to make it more authentic.

- Involve concerned persons to make the planning more accurate and error-free.

- The information system should be implemented appropriately, which gathers, processes, and makes reports of relevant data, and updates the reports more frequently to provide more real-time insights.

- You should be aware of current political and economic signals from government sectors to base your predictions more accurately.

There could be many other strategies specific to the problem that exists. The point here is that, of course, much like everything else in the universe, there are limitations to financial planning, but the advantages clearly supersede them. For a company to be able to do well and ensure a prosperous future, FP&A tends to play an enormous role.

Chapter 8 – How much of an Impact does FP&A have on a Company's Share Price?

Financial planning and analysis (FP&A) specialists are in charge of a company's financial planning, budgeting, and forecasting process, which helps the executive team and board of directors make critical decisions. These employees gather, prepare, and analyze financial data from all around the company to develop reports that provide data-driven answers to business concerns. The FP&A department is becoming more forward-thinking. It employs best practices to concentrate not just on what occurred or is occurring but also on why it is happening as well as what is expected to happen in the future.

In recent years, the function of FP&A has changed. FP&A analysts used to be solely concerned with recording and reporting financial outcomes and extrapolating future sales and earnings based on historical financial data. However, today's flow of data and the technology that helps analysts make sense of it has enabled FP&A to shift from reactive to proactive work, giving brilliant projections and analyses that directly impact the business's future. Financial analysts, unlike accountants, are in charge of studying, analyzing, and assessing the entirety of a corporation's financial activities and planning out the company's financial future. Income, spending, taxes, capital expenditures, investments, and financial statements are all under the supervision of FP&A professionals.

Professionals in financial planning and analysis conduct quantitative and qualitative analyses of all areas of a company's operations to assess its progress toward its objectives and to map out future goals and plans. FP&A analysts look at economic and business trends, analyze historical corporate performance, and try to predict hurdles and prospective difficulties to forecast a company's future financial results. Financial analysts are essentially building financial projects when they put together reports like three-year and five-year financial estimates. Good financial analysts frequently bring project management talents to the table, such as leadership, cost and time management, delegation, communication, and overall problem-solving abilities.

Individuals capable of handling and effectively evaluating a mountain of different forms of data and data evaluation measures are considered good financial analysts. Financial analysts are adept at resolving issues. They can decipher the other jigsaw pieces that make up a company's finances and envisage how to put them together to create several development scenarios.

FP&A professionals can help organizations in different ways. Firstly, they use the return on investment (ROI) and such comparisons with how the firm could use its cash flow to determine whether its current assets and investments are the best use of its excess working capital. Moreover, they also utilize vital financial statistics like the debt-to-equity ratio, current ratio, and interest coverage ratio to assess the company's overall financial health. FP&A professionals also work to figure out which of the company's goods or product lines generates the most net profit, and how these lines of businesses are performing when compared to peers. This makes them advise the organization in continuing or discontinuing a product. In addition to this, FP&A also compares past results to budgets and forecasts and performs variance analysis to explain performance variations and create future improvements. Last but not least, the most essential role of an FP&A professional is to Examine potential expansion or growth opportunities for the company. They Develop growth strategies that include capital expenditures and investments and create financial estimates for the next three to five years.

Now, I will discuss some essential financial statements for every FP&A team.

Necessary Financial Statements for Every FP&A Team.

Following financial statements is vital for every FP&A team to make financial projections.

Budget Variance Analysis

Budget variance analysis, also known as budget vs. actual variance analysis, is a classic FP&A procedure in which FP&A specialists compare real data from a specific period to the ones you planned. This vital financial reporting process is designed to give organizations visibility into revenue variances, actual expenses versus budget, and other deviations from their expectations and a foundation for more strategic questions. Each department has its own budget, which is in line with the organization's overall budget. Department heads must be able to see how their actual spending compares to their budget. A comparative report on the same is also necessary for the FP&A team.

Cashflow Forecasting

Estimating the flow of cash in and out of business over a set period is known as cash flow forecasting. An effective cash flow prediction allows companies to foresee future financial positions, avoid debilitating cash shortages, and maximize profits on any cash surpluses they may have. The FP&A teams analyze the organization's future liquidity by analyzing the company's current cash flow. This forecasting helps the organization address the cash flow issues early.

Executive Summary Reports & Dashboards Based on the Core Financial Statements

The three primary financial statements the company has at year-end are; the balance sheet, statement of cash flows, and income statement. So, the FP&A professionals thoroughly analyze these core financial statements and compare them with the statements of previous years to easily forecast the financial future of the company.

Operations Review Report

Sound operational controls are vital for the success of any organization. That is one of the reasons that FP&A

teams also examine operations reports. They assess the information and advise the management to improve their operational efficiency.

Members of the FP&A team are responsible for foretelling the company's profit and loss. In short, FP&A is a key ally in the definition and pursuit of operational targets and therefore company's target share price. The managers and directors of a company's FP&A team are providing realistic, rolling forecasts, and are responsible for sourcing, analyzing, and interpreting past performance, capital expenditures against ROI, and assessing contemporary and developing market trends. Management teams often provide these revenues and net income guidance to shareholders based on the budgets and forecasts prepared by FP&A teams. Getting the forecasts wrong not only will hinder the management team to allocate resources appropriately and therefore prevent achieving its strategic objectives, but it will also have a direct and immediate impact on a company's share price.

Further, they also ensure that operational obstructions are properly identified and that financial targets remain in sight. That also brings into light the sourcing of seasoned, savvy FP&A arm which is a crucial determinant of a company's operational success.

While a strategic plan outlines a company's direction, operational planning is an actual roadmap of getting there. This involves setting KPIs (key performance indicators) which help monitor company's operational performance and processes, and therefore ensures that the company is on the right track.

Chapter 9 – Upcoming Trends in Finance

The urge to adapt finance functions to the constantly shifting corporate environment is continual. Finance organizations have been casting a wider net for new efficiency opportunities, and boosting finance's role in managing data. In addition, there is a higher emphasis on advanced analytics-powered data-visualization techniques in order to facilitate decision-making.

Although there is no end in sight for this transformation, forward-thinking CFOs must be aware of what a productive, value-adding finance function will look like in a decade. In this chapter, I will briefly discuss the steps that organizations need to take to transform their finance department in accordance with the need of modern times.

Following are some of the ways through which CFOs can transform their organizations' finance departments.

Data and Processes Consolidation

Financial planning and analysis departments gather data through forecasting or income statements, while accounting may use general ledger data. Traditional finance operations may take data from numerous systems utilizing techniques specific to each system. However, irregular data generation and distribution from separate processes can prohibit analysts from delivering accurate planning and forecasting, lead to process inefficiencies, and raise the possibility of analytical errors.

An organization can consolidate and reconcile these processes, learn and automate transactions, and surface exceptions and anomalies by adopting an intelligent data core, which is relatively easy to adopt in current times through machine learning. Through machine learning, organizations can create a flexible data source that can process large volumes of financial, external, and operational information. These finance functions can take control of the data model and governance and lead an organization's transformation by implementing a flexible data core.

Looking beyond transactional activities, advanced computing power, machine learning, and artificial intelligence (AI) can be increasingly applied to complex tasks in order to automate transactional activities such as financial audits, risk management, and so on. Focus on big data over the last few years has resulted in increased demand for workers with analytical skills, such as data scientists and machine-learning engineers. As a result, finance organizations can now:

- Focus on high-end automation instead of low-end mature, first-wave automation approaches such as RPA. This "second-wave" automation can be applied for financial planning, audit, and capital allocation decisions.

- Align with enterprise-level AI and machine-learning technologies in a firmwide changing technology landscape in order to encourage collaboration between finance and other business units in an organization.

- Utilize FP&A's time effectively on analyses that drive actual business performance such as prescribing a future course of action instead of reactive analyses on historical data

Rely On Data Instead of Instincts

Making decisions that bring value to the business out of data insights is one of the crucial functions of a finance department. Accurate data can be collected and organized, but unless the finance department can analyze, evaluate, and effectively convey that data, it won't be used to its full, high-growth potential.

Traditionally, the finance departments of organizations rely on their instincts, especially during mergers and forecasting. However, this is not the case with modern finance departments. It is forecasted that the finance departments will not rely on their instincts by 2030. Instead, they will solely rely on the available data.

A carefully defined master data-management plan is necessary for finance departments to direct the collecting, archiving, and analysis of the ever-increasing volume of data required to carry out the many sorts of analytics the business demands. The finance department must be able to quickly gather reliable, high-quality data to support the business—whether through more complex financial scenario modeling, knowledge of how to better manage liquidity, or better advice on how to effectively invest assets.

Building and managing data clouds that comprise general-ledger financial data, inventory data, sales data, HR data, and a variety of external business information is something FP&A teams do in collaboration with IT and other operational units of the business. This makes it simple for FP&A teams to compile data points and provide them to business executives responsible for enhancing key performance indicators in real time. Comparatively to peer businesses, FP&A teams are more likely to combine financial and non-financial data to produce a consistent fact basis that can support essential business decisions and enhance organizational performance.

Due to the finance function's unique position in a central role, it can help consolidate, simplify and control company-wide data. This can be done through:

- Setting high standards on data structure, aggregation, storage, and security firmwide. FP&A professionals can also take a larger role in driving enterprise-wide transformation efforts. This can be further expanded to other business units through unified collaboration with IT, digital, and other operational functions.

- Preserving a single source of truth to data while adopting of a layered architecture by investing in a tech-enabled agile data structure.

- Invest in validation and clean-up of data at the point of entry, as well as resolving data-quality issues by understanding existing data limitations. Finance organizations can utilize machine-learning algorithms which can help cross-reference and validate data, and reduce manual errors.

Efficient and Diverse Workforce

Intelligent and efficient finance departments will diversify the positions and skill sets they're looking for. With improved financial insights and more expansive strategic thinking, CFOs are becoming more integrated into the C-suite. Many leaders recognize a broader shift in demands and skills. This change is fueled by talent with experience in those fields. It is dependent on technologies like artificial intelligence and predictive analytics.

Reducing reliance on the IT function is necessary to maintain operations and insights within the financial organization. This is a crucial shift that finance directors will need to undertake if they want to take advantage of new digital capabilities. We are already seeing different departments start to recruit data scientists for their requirements. Though tech-savvy employees will be in high demand, traditional finance abilities remain crucial. Finance executives can promote rotations and other training opportunities for the current personnel.

The finance department should be strengthened by hiring individuals with strong business acumen who can analyze large amounts of financial data and make wise judgments while always keeping in mind the overall strategic aims of the company. Future financial professionals will have a more significant impact on how strategy is developed. Therefore, they must have a deeper awareness of potential opportunities and hazards.

Precise Decision Making

The finance leaders should encourage the FP&A professionals to utilize modern technological tools to make precise financial decisions on time such as using advanced analytics to improve cash-flow forecasting. This will save the organization from future losses. It will also help companies capitalize on their investments at the right time.

FP&A is also responsible for aiding the firm's performance discussions and recommending the best course of action to improve performance, revenue, profits, and so on. For this purpose, finance professionals need to provide:

- Clear insights by highlighting shortfalls against expected outcomes along with underlying factors causing those gaps.

- Rich insights by incorporating more robust datasets from a wider variety of external sources. By leveraging both internal and external datasets, FP&A can help provide a more realistic view of performance outcomes and better simulate multiple scenarios.

- Faster insights in order for management to change its trajectory quickly and decisively.

Chapter 10 – The Exit Strategy

I have discussed the career opportunities that FP&A offers to its professionals in previous chapters. By now, we all are well aware that FP&A careers are lucrative and offer attractive salary packages along with different perks and benefits. Now, in this chapter, I will discuss how much an FP&A professional can achieve after reaching the Director or Vice-President (VP) level.

FP&A Exit Opportunities

After reaching the rank of Director/VP, the majority of FP&A specialists tend to stay in the field, either within their present company or at other firms. Most directors start to look after the more significant responsibilities relating to the organization's financial health, such as the

P&L or Balance Sheet of the organization at a macro level. These directors are promoted vertically since they look after greater responsibilities than their other counterparts, making them more deserving of extra pay and benefits.

Chief Financial Officer (CFO)

Another alternative is to become a Chief Financial Officer (CFO) of the organization. However, with only a single vacancy available, becoming a CFO is pretty rare for every FP&A professional. FP&A professionals seeking this advancement often look to other essential departments within the organization, such as Controller, Business Development, Corporate Development, and Operations, to gain the well-rounded skill sets needed to match the CFO position's criteria.

Chief Executive Officer (CEO)

Some FP&A professionals even excel in the position of the Chief Executive Officer (CEO) of the organization. However, the chances of an FP&A professional becoming a CEO are rarer than becoming a CFO. Those who aspire to become CEOs often start their own businesses and take the entrepreneurial path in order to achieve the highest position in any organization.

Investment Banking

Since FP&A professionals deal with numbers throughout their careers, they have bright chances of becoming successful in investment banking. Some FP&A professionals go into investment banking or private equity after reaching the director's position in their FP&A career. However, it has been noted that a tiny percentage of FP&A professionals opt for this exit strategy after they reach the top.

The other and most feasible exit opportunities for FP&A professionals are present in corporate finance. Let's first discuss what exactly is meant by corporate finance and what are the exit opportunities for FP&A professionals in this sector.

Corporate Finance

Corporate finance deals with how organizations deal with their investment decisions, funding in the right places, and capital structure through long and short-term financial planning. Furthermore, it also implies implementing these various financial strategies within the organization.

Following are some of the main exit opportunities for FP&A professionals in corporate finance.

Controllership

Controllership is considered the most boring job in the finance sector by some. The reason behind it is that the job requires the incumbent to inspect journal entries throughout the day, causing redundancy and boredom at the workplace. However, another side of the story illustrates that not only controllership job is thrilling; instead, it is high paying as well.

Controllership puts the incumbent the in-charge of balance sheet integrity. In simple words, it means that the controller has to provide solutions to the balance sheet integrity-related problems that may include misstatements, cash, bank, and inventory reconciliation, financial risk mitigation, and ensuring that the organization is complying with the guidelines of regulators. The controller works with the internal audit teams to ensure compliance and therefore save the organization from the regulator's penalties. As a controller, the job of an FP&A professional is to ensure accounting accuracy, along with keeping the CFO happy by following their instruction regarding aggressive or non-aggressive accounting. It is tough but a very high-paying job.

Treasury

Treasury is one of the most essential departments of any organization. It looks after the cash flow and ensures that the company should have enough in its reserve that is required for its survival.

It is a well-known fact that net income can be manipulated in different ways. One can find many case studies in this regard as well. The organizations manipulate their net income to gain investors' confidence. However, one cannot manipulate the amount of cash that the organization generates or losses. This makes the treasury job challenging as it deals solely with the cash flow.

While working in treasury, the FP&A professionals forecast the cash needs of the organization to save the company from any liquidity crisis in the future. Their job is to ensure that the required cash is available at the organization's disposal.

The FP&A professionals utilize different methods to make the required cash available for the organization. They raise equity, release bonds, or negotiate with the banks for the extension of credit lines. They have to stay in constant contact with investors and banks to meet the cash requirements of their organization.

Similarly, to ensure that the company does not face a liquidity crunch in the future, the FP&A professionals also advise the organization to invest in different short-term funds. It helps organizations to earn profits from their idle money.

Working in a treasury is a very high-paying job. A senior analyst at treasure easily earns between $ 170k - $ 180k per annum.

Some people also move into a more strategic and commercial role depending on their individual interests.

Lastly, one can also transition into a management consulting or operational consulting career, as Financial Planning & Analysis really teaches you a lot about strategy, as well as it's execution and implementation.

Made in the USA
Coppell, TX
26 August 2023